PARABLES OF THE BIBLE

PARABLES OF THE BIBLE
The Sheep That Was Found

Drejervej 15,3 DK-2400 Copenhagen NV, Denmark
Tel.: (+45) 3531 0330 Fax: (+45) 3531 0334
E-mail: info@scanpublishing.dk
Website: www.scanpublishing.dk

Design by Ben Alex
Printed in China
ISBN 87 7247 779 2 (Hard cover)
ISBN 87 7247 774 1 (Soft cover)

PARABLES OF THE BIBLE

THE SHEEP THAT WAS FOUND

Luke 15:1—7

Illustrations by
Gustavo Mazali

scandinavia

The kind shepherd

There once was a man who was taking care of sheep. He was called a shepherd. The shepherd was a good man who loved his sheep and took good care of them.

Wild animals

Sometimes wild beasts like lions and wolves would attack the sheep. But the shepherd was brave. He fought them off and stayed with his sheep. He never left his sheep on their own.

A missing lamb

One day, a little lamb wandered away from the others and got lost in the wilderness. At the end of the day the shepherd noticed one was missing. He looked around, but no little lamb in sight. So he made sure the other sheep were safe in the fold. Then he went out to look for the lost lamb.

The shepherd calling

The shepherd searched for a long time. He called and called for the missing lamb. But still no lamb in sight. He went deeper into the wilderness. He wouldn't give up. He was determined to find his lost lamb.

Lost in the desert

Finally the shepherd heard a "Baaa" far away. He followed the sound and saw the missing lamb stuck in a thorn bush. The lamb pulled and pulled but couldn't free itself. All it could was cry out "Baaa" and wait. The shepherd hurried over to rescue his lamb.

The lamb is found

The shepherd bent down and picked up the lamb. Then he put it on his shoulders and carefully carried it home to safety. The shepherd was very happy. The lamb that was lost had finally been found.

The sheep that was found

—read the story in the Bible

Now the tax collectors and "sinners" were all gathering around to hear him. But the Pharisees and the teachers of the law muttered, "This man welcomes sinners and eats with them."

Then Jesus told them this parable: "Suppose one of you has a hundred sheep and loses one of them. Does he not leave the ninety-nine in the open country and go after the lost sheep until he finds it? And when he finds it, he joyfully puts it on his shoulders and goes home. Then he calls his friends and neighbors together and says, 'Rejoice with me; I have found my lost sheep.' I tell you that in the same way there will be more rejoicing in heaven over one sinner who repents than over ninety-nine righteous persons who do not need to repent."

Luke 15:1-7